A DICTIONARY FOR THE SPORT PARACHUTIST

skydiving

A DICTIONARY FOR THE SPORT PARACHUTIST

Written and Illustrated by
Bill FitzSimons

Bandit Books
Winston-Salem, North Carolina

Library of Congress Catalog Card Number 90-84620
ISBN 1-878177-01-X

Bandit Books
P.O. Box 11721
Winston-Salem, North Carolina 27106
(919) 785-7417

First Bandit Books Edition: November 1990

Manufactured in the United States of America

DISCLAIMER

The material presented herein is total nonsense. Anyone who
takes this book seriously does so at his own risk.

*To all those who have committed their frail bodies
to the unrelenting gravity of the wild blue.*

A

A License	The skydiver with an A (basic) license has advanced beyond the student phase, and is able to jumpmaster himself, perform basic relative work jumps, pack his own parachute, and tie his own shoe laces.
Accelerated Freefall	A program of instruction in which the skydiving novice begins his training with freefall, moving rapidly toward relative work skills, poverty, and divorce.
Accident Report	Any report in a skydiving journal which analyzes a parachuting accident in such a way that the cause is clearly shown to be human carelessness, and to have no inherent relationship to the sport of skydiving.
AGL	Above Ground Level. Skydivers and jump pilots should always refer to altitude "above ground level," and not mean "mean sea level." For that matter, you shouldn't even be jumping above sea level. You want to get drowned? (See Water Jump)
Altimeter	One of a number of distracting devices available to the parachutist to provide information about his impending doom.
Arch	1. What students do with their backs, when they first learn how to jump, so they'll stay stable. 2. The leader of the Miller Lite Six-Pack Skydiving Team.

Automatic Opening Device

A device which will open the reserve parachute automatically at a preset altitude, in the event the jumper for any reason neglects to do so himself, and at other times as well.

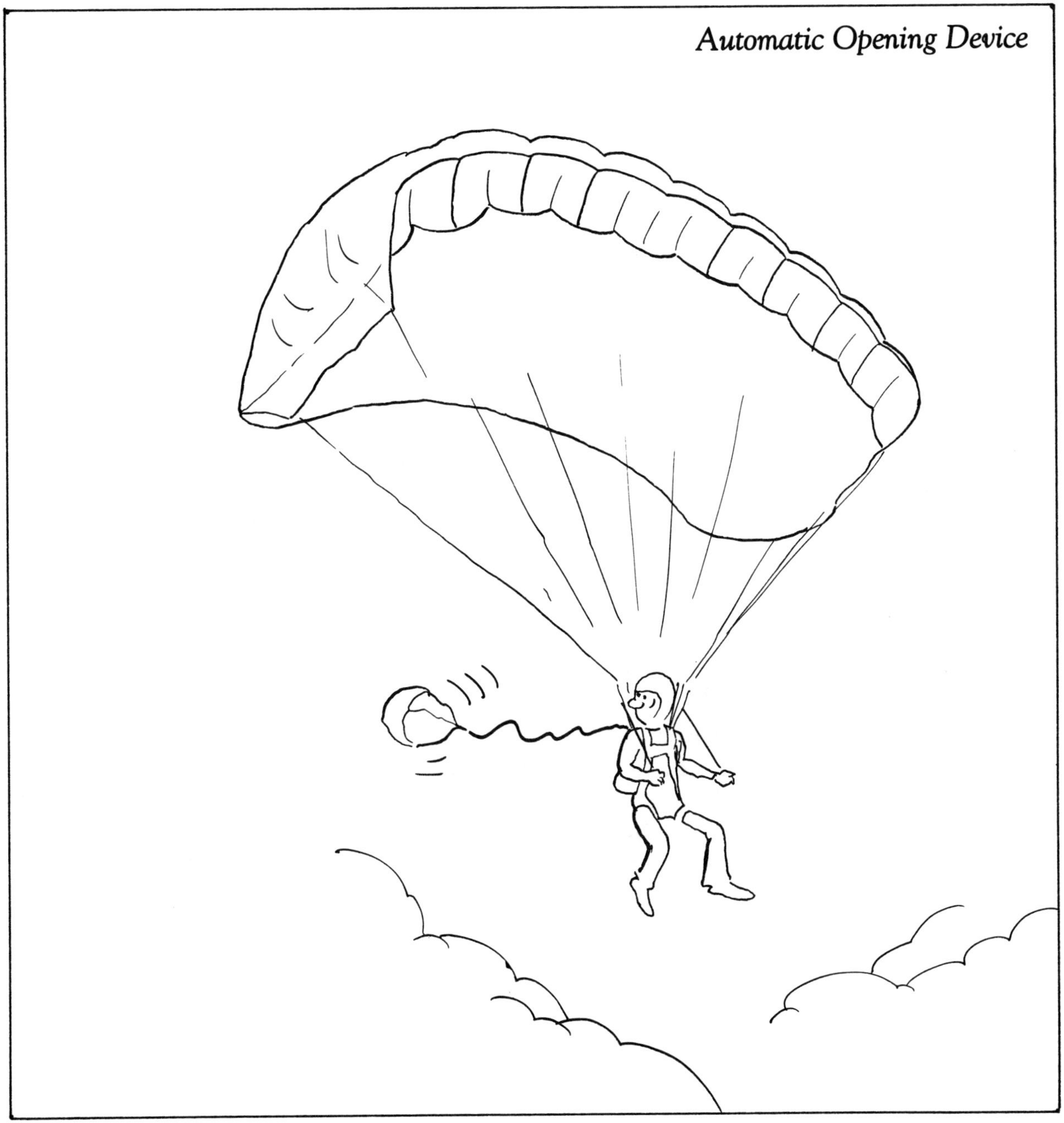
Automatic Opening Device

B

B license	The holder of the B (intermediate) license has met the requirements for the A license, but has not yet achieved those goals necessary for the C license. (This was true, even before the license requirements were changed, and while this definition may not be very helpful, it will save needless revisions to the dictionary, and is probably all you really need to know.)
Base Jumping	A new sport derived from skydiving, the purpose of which is to make skydiving seem relatively sensible. "BASE" is actually an acronym. To qualify for a base number, and be certifiable, base jumpers must make at least one jump from four different locations: A balcony **(B)**, an apple tree **(A)**, a staircase **(S)**, and an emporium **(E)**. (See Russian Roulette)
BGL	Below Ground Level. Where you'll be if you don't open your parachute at the proper altitude above ground level.
Boogie	An extended skydiving party distinguished by the large number of participants, excessive consumption of food and drink, and an abundance of aircraft.

Bounce	Originally, an event in Polish skydiving in which the contestants landed on the drop zone without deploying either parachute. The jumper who bounced the highest was declared the winner. For this event a special rig was developed, the well-known Polish parachute, which opens on impact. Today this term applies to any landing that is performed in that old-world manner.
Breakaway	If a skydiver has a partial malfunction, and there is the danger of entanglement with the reserve parachute, he may perform a "break-away," which involves pulling a release handle to disconnect the parachute from the harness. This should really be called a release, or a fallaway, but they call it a breakaway. Some people call it a cutaway, which is even more stupid, if you ask me. If you tell somebody you did a "cutaway," they always think you cut the goddamned risers with a knife. (For what it's worth, I don't make up these words, just the definitions.)
Breakoff Altitude	This is a predetermined altitude at which relative work parachutists agree to stop their relative work and turn their attention to tracking away and opening their parachutes. For CRW, the breakoff altitude is where the participants agree to give up trying to untangle their wraps and breakaway (cutaway) to their reserves. Thirty-five hundred feet, for example, is a good breakoff altitude, while seven hundred feet leaves something to be desired. Breakoff altitude should always be AGL, not MSL, and definitely not BGL.

Bridge Day	An annual, one-day event held at the New River Bridge near Fayettteville, West Virginia, in which parachutists from all over the world gather to make parachute jumps from an 876 foot bridge, into a rocky river. Really bright, huh? Microbiologists have traced this strange urge to a defective gene, recessive in most humans, but dominant in a few skydivers and a small rodent called a lemming.
BSRs	The "R" stands for requirements, and we all know what BS is, right, gang? But, seriously, the BSRs represent common-sense (basic safety) standards that we all love and abide by.

C

C License	Skydivers holding the USPA C (advanced) license have advanced beyond the B license requirements, and can do all sorts of impressive things, only they don't have their D license yet, so they're not so hot.
Canopy	That part of the parachute what do the decelerating, given a proper deployment and opening.
Canopy Relative Work	Sometimes called simply CRW, this is the latest space-age way to kill yourself. Participants actually entangle themselves in each other's suspension lines and canopies to make a formation, and then see how long they can fly the formation before they have an irreversible entanglement, which is called a wrap.
Canopy Release	Any gizmo the purpose of which is to release the parachute canopy and risers from the harness, in case of a malfunction or, on the ground, if you are being dragged by the wind. Use your own good judgment.

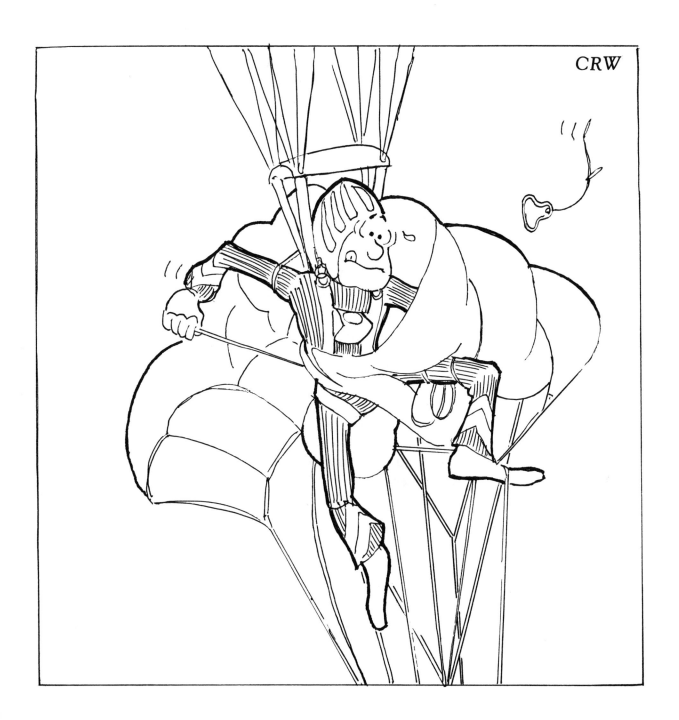

Chest Mounted Reserve	Also called the front mounted reserve and the belly wart, this is a reserve packed in its own container, which is then hooked onto the parachute harness on the jumper's chest, so that when it malfunctions he can see it as soon as it happens. In the old days, this was the only type of reserve container available. The modern rig has the reserve mounted on the back, so that if you have a total malfunction of your reserve, there's nothing you can do about it.
Clear and Pull	A parachute jump in which the parachutist pulls his ripcord (or throws out his pilot chute) as soon as he clears the aircraft. Also called a hop-and-pop, but not to be confused with a jump-and-hump.
Connector Links	Connector links are hardware devices used to attach parachute suspension lines to the risers. Risers, in turn, are attached to the parachute harness, and are made just long enough so that the connector links can bang into the parachutist's head as the parachute deploys. Today's connector links are little tiny gadgets called rapid links, and you can buy bumpers to put on them, to protect your head.
Container	Everybody knows this one, so I won't go into it.
Cooper	D.B. Cooper, the "Johnny Appleseed" of skydiving, is the only person ever to have achieved national fame through parachuting. In one daring leap, this outlaw parachutist spread twenty-dollar bills and, apparently, himself, over the great Northwest.

Crossport	A crossport is a hole cut or burned into the ribs of a ram-air canopy to provide even air pressure inside the canopy and prevent collapsed end cells. So named because they were first used in Crossport, Connecticut.
Cut	When the pilot is on jump run, the jumpmaster looks out the door, giving the pilot any necessary corrections, such as, "five (degrees) left," or "ten right," or sometimes, "I don't even see the fuckin' drop zone." When it's time for the jumpers to position themselves for the exit, the jumpmaster will scream, "cut!" This is the pilot's cue to begin his stall recovery practice, slowing the aircraft so the jumpers don't get blown away. It's all very exciting.
Cutaway	1. What the rescue squad does to your clothes when you have a compound fracture. 2. Emergency parachute release. (See Breakaway)

Cut

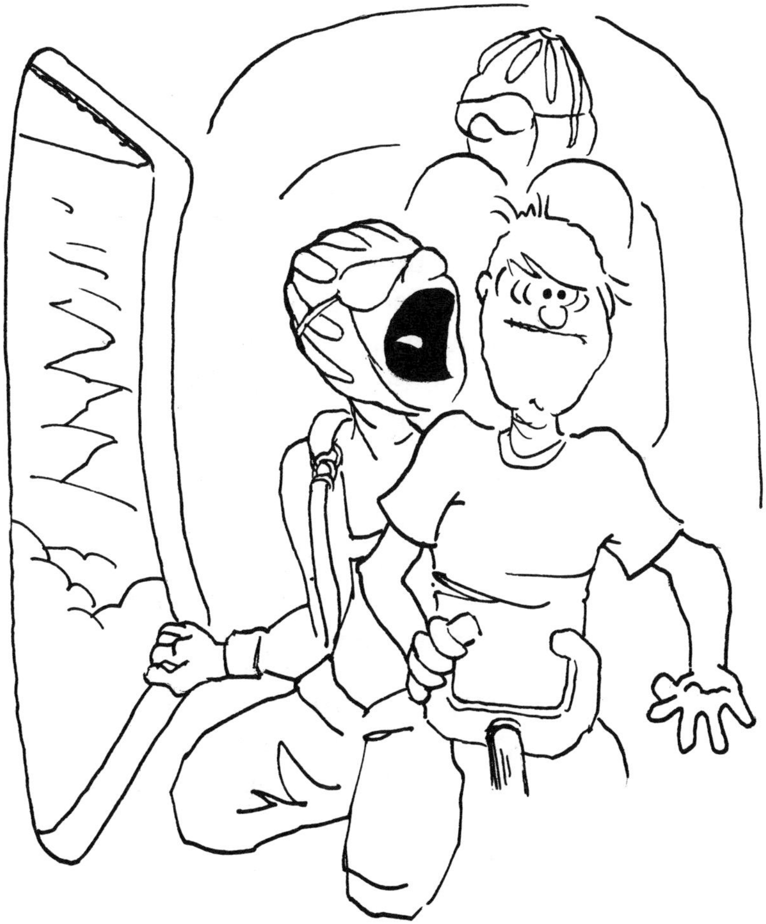

D

D License	The highest USPA license you can get. Once you've got your D license, you are a "Master Skydiver." If you have a D license, you can do just about anything you want to, although in some situations, like with the state police and the father of a fifteen year old girl, it takes a bit of explaining.
Dead Center	An accuracy landing in which the parachutist touches down on a small disk, usually in a pit filled with pea gravel. Jumpers in the early days of accuracy frequently killed themselves in the process of getting a dead center, hence the name.
Delay	In skydiver talk, a delay is how long you take before you open your parachute, and is best coordinated with the altitude of the jump. You might take a ten-second delay, or a thirty-second delay, or even a sixty-second delay. A forty-five minute delay is almost always too long.
Demo	A parachute jump, performed for an audience, for which the participants are paid a sum of money. Demo jumpers usually wear some sort of costume, such as a clown suit, a Santa outfit, or combat fatigues and steel helmet.

Demo

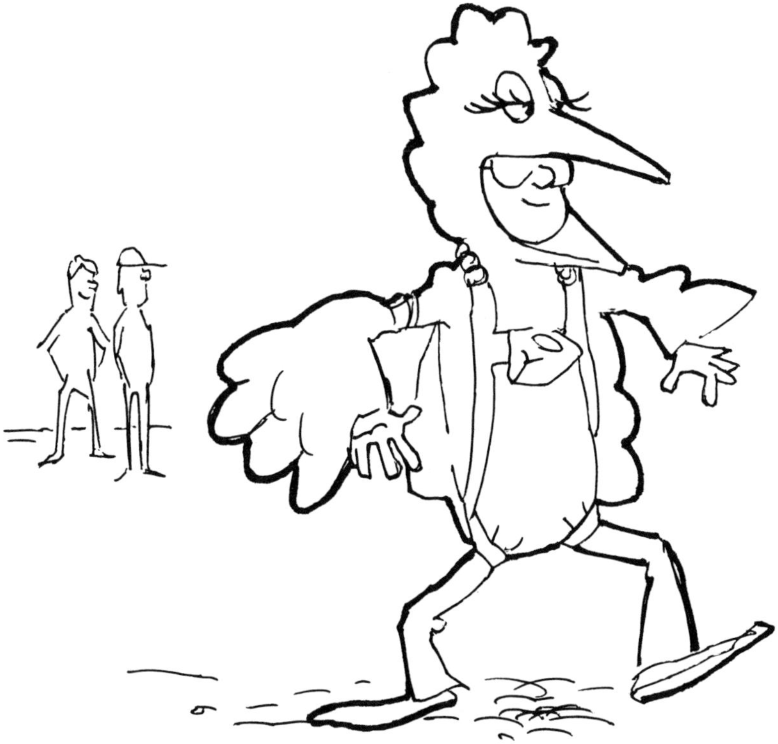

Deployment	Deployment means the parachute is out of the container, and the suspension lines are stretched out, but the canopy is not yet inflated. You can have a perfectly normal deployment and still have a streamer or a partial malfunction. Still, deployment is a good thing, because in order to have a good opening you first must have a good deployment. It all happens very fast, so you don't even have to think about it, if you don't want to.
Deployment Bag	The deployment bag is what holds the canopy during the first stages of deployment. You've got to have a deployment, so you've got to have a bag, right? Figure at least thirty or forty bucks for a deployment bag. (As you will have noticed by now, anything you need in the way of miscellaneous parachute gear is going to cost at least thirty or forty dollars, and it goes up from there.)
Diaper	A square cloth you pin around a baby's ass.
Dirt Dive	A rehearsal, on the ground, of maneuvers the participants have no hope of ever completing, performed for the amusement of fellow skydivers and to impress any whuffos who may have strayed onto the drop zone.
Divorce	The legal action taken by a skydiver's spouse once he or she finds out what goes on at the drop zone.
Docking	A skydiver who successfully approaches and enters a freefall or CRW formation is said to have docked. To be considered successful, the docking skydiver must not destroy the formation, and all participants must remain conscious, or regain consciousness within three seconds.

Door Exit	This is when the skydiver just bombs out of the door of the aircraft, without regard to stability or common courtesy. Not to be confused with the "window exit," which usually follows a premature opening, which is not to be confused with premature ejaculation. Next definition!
Down Plane	A jump aircraft that has stalled on takeoff or jump run.
Drop Zone	A location for dropping controlled substances which have been flown into the country from south of the border. A skydiving school is frequently operated at these fields.
Dummy Ripcord Pull	A static line jump in which a dummy (student) practices pulling a phony rip cord, just to prove that he really can do it while maintaining stability. The jumpmaster watches from the aircraft to be certain that the pull is successful, because you can never trust a student. The student, on the other hand, always trusts the jumpmaster, because he (the student) is a dummy, right? Doesn't this all sound familiar?

Down Plane

E

El Capitan	A religious shrine in California. Every faithful base jumper must make a jump from El Capitan at least once in his life. The mountain is also a shrine to the U. S. Park Police, who must arrest at least one base jumper to qualify for their retirement pension.
Emergency Parachute	A certificated parachute for emergency use, just like a reserve parachute, except that you only wear the one parachute because you're not a skydiver, you just don't trust the airplane. Like, the jump pilot wears an emergency parachute, because even though he's not a skydiver, he did the preflight, and he knows a potential emergency when he sees one.
Equipment	This term applies to every item that the parachutist might require, and may vary from skydiver to skydiver. Items of equipment include the unusual, such as sophisticated automatic opening devices, and the everyday items, such as gloves, underwear, and a sixpack of Budweiser.
Exhibition Jump	A demonstration jump made by exhibitionists, the exhibition jump being made in the nude. Prostitutes who make an official exhibition jump should have a "PRO" rating.

Exhibition Jump

Exit	The exit is the actual jump, or departure from the aircraft in flight. From the Latin "exire," to jump from a noisy and poorly maintained machine.
Exit Point	The exact location above the ground where, if you had only got out of the aircraft there, you could make it back to the field.

F

FAA An official agency of the United States Department of Transportation, the FAA is responsible for safety in the sky. Their no-nonsense approach to this task is to discourage, as much as possible, any activity that includes flying or using the airspace in any way.

FAI Federation Aeronautique Internationale, ze international organization which governs all ze aviation sports, certifies all ze official aviation and space records, and governs official international competitions. Zat kind of thing.

Fatality An accident that seriously curtails one's future skydiving activity.

Flare 1. What the parachutist does, just before touching down, to produce a perfect, soft, stand-up landing. 2. What the rescue squad uses to help the Medical Evac Helicopter find the drop zone, if the parachutist misjudges the flare.

Flotation Device A device, attached to the harness of a parachutist making a water jump, to help the rescue squad locate the body downstream.

Free Bag A reserve deployment bag that helps to prevent horseshoe malfunctions. When an equipment dealer advertises a rig, complete with free bag, the free bag usually costs you an extra sixty to seventy-five dollars.

Freefall Photographer

Freefall	That part of a parachute jump before deployment, when the parachutist is "falling free." Initially, the jumper accelerates at thirty-two feet per second, per second. (Author's note: If you ever figure out what the hell that means, please let me know.) Freefall usually costs in excess of one dollar per thousand feet of altitude, and is therefore about as free as the "free bag" defined above.
Freefall Photographer	A skydiving masochist whose interests are parachuting, photography, and whiplash.
Freestyle	An artistic and aesthetically pleasing attempt by an unstable parachutist in freefall to regain stability.
French Boots	Parachute boots, once popular with skydivers, which provided support and protection to the ankle by transferring all stress of impact, and likelihood of fracture, to the leg.
French Helmet	A fashionable leather helmet that offers virtually no protection from impact, and probably could not be made to look sillier by the most determined French designer. The helmet makes the skydiver look like he has a pointed head, or maybe the manufacturer is really on to something. Anyhow, skydivers love them.
Frog Position	A relaxed but stable freefall position developed by the French. It is call a frog position, presumably, because a skydiver in this position looks like a frog in freefall, although I personally have never seen a frog in freefall, but you never know.

Freestyle

Ft. Benning, Georgia	A southern drop zone where the discipline is severe and the average student spends a hell of a long time on static line. Good rates, though.
Funnel	The end result of a high-speed, free-style, docking maneuver that has yet to gain widespread popularity.

G

Garbage Load

A group of skydivers who *know* they're about to waste their money.

Glide Ratio

The mathematical relationship between the vertical descent of a gliding device and its forward motion. For example, a canopy that descends ten feet for every one foot of forward motion is said by the manufacturer to have a glide ratio of three to one.

Gloves

Skydiving gloves are worn by parachutists for protection from injury and from the cold. A really good pair of skydiving gloves is very expensive, light weight and comfortable, and lasts about three weeks.

Goggles

Goggles should be worn by the skydiver to keep his eyeballs from drying out, and to keep foreign material and other shit from getting in his eyes.

Gold Wings

A gold badge awarded to a skydiver who has made one thousand freefall parachute jumps, this little pin costs about ten or fifteen thousand dollars.

Golden Knights

An elite team of U. S. Army paratroopers whose job it is to demonstrate to the public that our armed forces can seek out and develop skills which have absolutely nothing to do with national defense. (See Leapfrog)

Ground Rush
The visual illusion experienced by parachutists in free-fall, when they are approaching the ground. As the jumper goes low, objects on the ground appear to rush away from him in all directions. When he hits the ground, objects *do* rush away from him in all directions.

H

HALO	HALO is an acronym for "High Altitude, Low Opening." This is a military jump, complete with oxygen bail-out bottles, for the purpose of landing a few men behind enemy lines. I don't think it's a very good idea, myself. I mean, for one thing, you're outnumbered before you even begin to shoot people. I don't get it.
Hardware	Any metallic device used in parachuting which, in practical use, leaves a mark on the human body that lasts for more than forty-eight hours.
Harness	That item of equipment consisting of straps and hardware used to attach the parachute assembly to the human body in such a manner that the opening shock and subsequent weight loading are spread uniformly throughout the genital area. The modern harness and container can be thought of as a single unit; however, this is not mandatory, and you can think of it any way you like. Besides, as Socrates once asked, "Does thinking make it so?"
Helmet	Fashionable headgear worn by some parachutists.
Hockey Helmet	Favored by some parachutists, the hockey helmet represents a compromise between safety and style: it is inadequate enough to be considered fashonable, but still provides protection from freefall collision with a hockey puck.

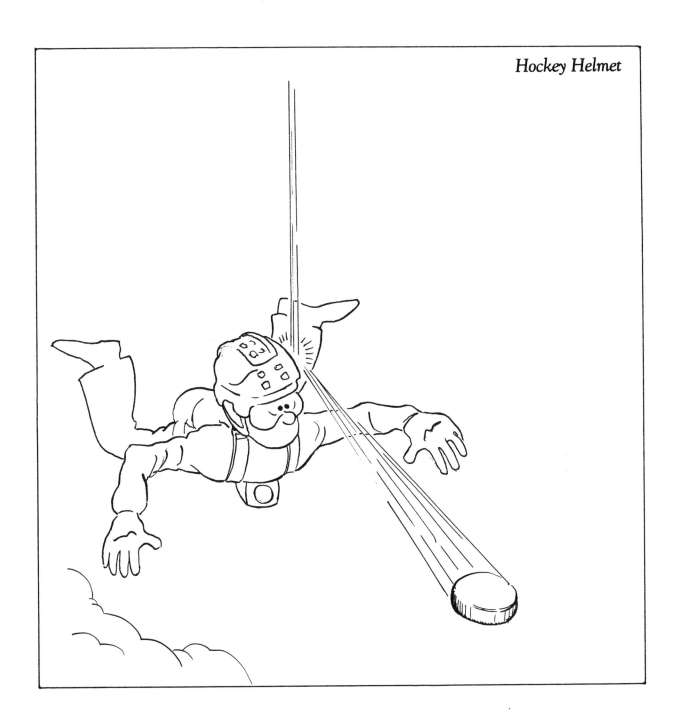

Horseshoe Malfunction	This is a malfunction in which the pilot chute becomes snagged on the parachutist, and the canopy and lines deploy, kind of, only the parachute can't inflate because it's still upside down, stuck to the jumper. The whole mess somewhat resembles an upside-down horse shoe, and everybody knows that if you nail a horseshoe on your barn door upside down, all the luck will run out. If you have a horseshoe malfunction, you'll think all your luck has run out, too.
Hypoxia	Hypoxia is oxygen deficiency experienced at higher altitudes, and can result in impaired judgment, unconsciousness, and death. This is a serious threat to skydivers, who spend a lot of time at high altitudes, and whose judgment is not too keen to begin with. Supplemental oxygen is recommended for high altitude jumps, and even at lower altitudes, it couldn't hurt.

I

IFR	A less-than-perfect flight condition in which jump pilots must be coaxed into flying up through perfectly good holes in the cloud cover to attain proper jump altitude.
Inflation	The is the final phase of the parachute opening. First you have the pull, then the deployment, and finally the inflation. Once you've got a proper inflation, you're home free, unless, of course, you bust yourself up, landing.
	Inflation also means something about when the government prints too much money, and then prices go up, but that has nothing to do with skydiving (where the prices *always* go up), and I don't really understand it, so forget I even mentioned it.
Instructor	A skygod with a U.S.P.A. rating.

J

Jumpmaster	A qualified skydiver who assumes responsibility for all jumpers on the aircraft. Also called the "spotter," and "that son-of-a-bitch who put me out, two miles over the swamp."
Jump Suit	A one-piece suit of clothing designed to make you fall faster or slower, depending on the fashion this year, but always to look extremely silly, proving the old theory that form follows function.

K

Knife
A special and important piece of equipment carried by all serious skydivers. If a jumper becomes in any way intangled with suspension lines, the knife may be used to cut his wrists; in the event of an off-field landing, it will serve as a survival tool, and may be used to defend against hostile farmers. (Note: The skydivers' hook knife is designed to be safe, and cuts suspension lines easily, but it's a bitch to whittle with, and not at all practical for removing splinters from your finger.)

L

Leapfrog	A sailor with unbelievably good duty (See Golden Knight).
Leonardo da Vinci (1452 - 1519)	Inventor of the square parachute, this Italian genius was never successful in marketing his creation, probably because he never thought of cross-porting, never came up with a practical means of attaching the suspension lines, and was reluctant to provide packing tabs.
License	A skydiving license (A, B, C, or D) is issued by the USPA to parachutists who meet certain qualifications. Then there's the driver's license, and a business license, and James Bond has a license to kill, so it can be 'most anything.
Lie	A subjective variation of the truth, the lie is an indispensible tool to the skydiver who has just made a bad spot, blown a formation, or missed an alimony payment. It is also useful in describing one's previous accomplishments. Camus tells us that everybody lies. What's important is to lie well. Most skydivers understand this and have perfected the technique.
Log Book	A book with blank pages in which skydivers, when they are not jumping, sharpen their creative fiction writing abilities. For those jumpers who can't write, there are little rubber stamps to make pictures, which can then be colored on rainy days.

Leonardo da Vinci

M

Mae West

This is a partial malfunction of a round canopy, and is also called a "line over," but what it is, really, is a partial inversion. What happens, see, is that when the canopy deploys, but is not yet inflated (remember, we talked about this), a part of the skirt of the canopy blows through the lines on the other side, catches some air, and inflates in the wrong place. O.K., you say, so what does that have to do with Mae West? Well, it seems that a partial inversion looks a little like a woman's brassiere (a *big* woman), and the first American paratroopers, who for the most part had been bottle fed, decided to name this malfunction after an actress, Mae West, who had big Winnebagos that were much on their minds at the time. So you see, boys and girls, since the earliest days parachutists have been obsessed with self-gratification of one kind or another.

Malfunction

The failure of the main parachute to deploy and/or function as it normally should. A malfunction is usually followed quickly by the relief of any constipation the jumper may have been suffering, a few choice expletives, and the deployment of the reserve parachute.

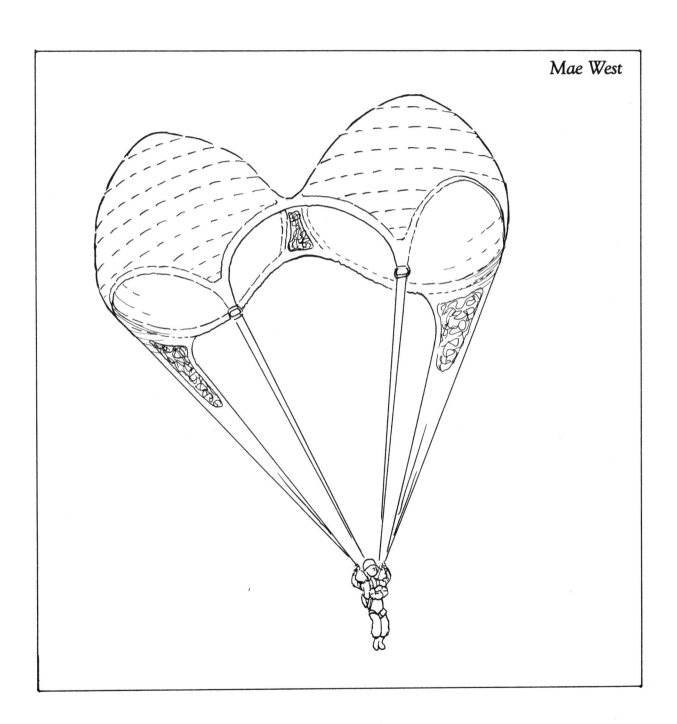

Max Track	A max track is like a regular track, except that it is just about the fastest, most efficient track you can get yourself into. Your body becomes a streamlined aerodynamic lifting device, and you go like hell, burning a hole through the sky without even looking where you're going. The Max Track was developed by a German, Max Niedemeyer, but he was denied a patent and now lives in poverty in a small village in Bavaria.
Modified Frog	Any frog that has been altered or in any way significantly changed.
Muskogee	Muskogee, Oklahoma, home of the National Skydiving Championships. Muskogee was chosen because of its location in the center of the contiguous United States, but primarily because it is geographically located in the windiest place in North America, the wind providing a challenge to accuracy jumpers. No one really knows why Oklahoma is so windy, but local residents claim it is because Kansas blows, and Texas sucks.

N

N.T.S.B.	These letters stand for the National Transportation Safety Board, a government agency whose job it is to perform a thorough investigation of any aviation accident. These dedicated public servants will not rest until, by meticulous investigation, they have uncovered conclusive evidence of pilot error.
Night Jump	A parachute jump made one hour after official sunset and one hour before official sunrise. Two night jumps are required for the advanced "D" license. Those parachutists who cannot arrange to have an official sun observer verify the existence of a nighttime condition may fulfill this requirement by making the same jumps during the day, but must promise to keep their eyes closed.
Nylon	Nylon is a synthetic material that was developed in 1932 by W. H. Carothers. He didn't think much of it at the time, but his supervisor realized the potential, immediately. "W. H.," he said, "you're going to change ladies' underwear." Well, of course, Carothers was delighted, and the rest of this story is history. Originally, parachutes, like ladies' underwear, were made of silk, which was prohibitively expensive. Then it was discovered that parachutes made of nylon were stronger, lighter, and more durable than those made of silk, and nylon became prohibitively expensive. It remains so today, as does everything else that is really fun.

Night Jump

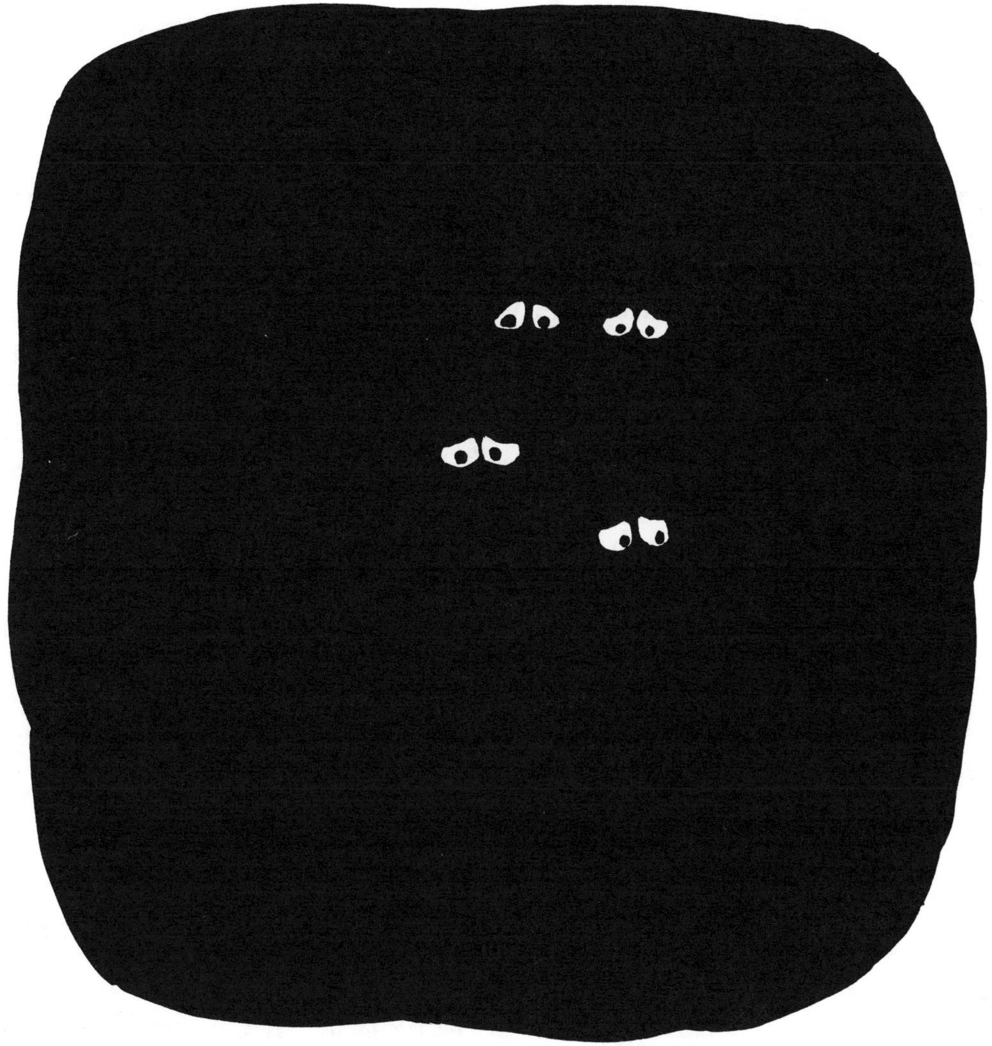

O

Open Body of Water	A body of water in which a skydiver might drown upon landing in it. Of course, he might not drown, but it's still an open body of water. He just might not be so lucky next time. The key to this definition is that it's all hypothetical. A friend of mine once drowned after landing, head first, in a toilet bowl, when he fell off the sink in a hotel room. The U.S.P.A. refused to acknowledge that this was a skydiving fatality, even though it was a skydiving party, the toilet seat was up, and the poor bastard did, in fact, drown. The Board of Directors did, however, after much litigation, admit that a toilet bowl is an open body of water, *provided* that the lid *and* the seat are in the upright position.
Opening Shock	The average parachutist's amazement when his parachute, which he packs in seven minutes, actually opens. Not to be confused with "Opening Force," which is the amount of energy, measured in calories, required to remove a stubborn top from a bottle of Coors.
Oscillation	If the parachutist is swinging back and forth under his canopy, that is oscillation. In Canopy Relative Work, it's the same thing, except it's caused by one of the other guys.

Ottley	Bill Ottley, the only living skydiver who actually knew Leonardo da Vinci.
Over Gross	Aeronautical term for the condition of a jump aircraft at take-off, and any skydiver after consuming two six-packs of beer and a pastrami sandwich.

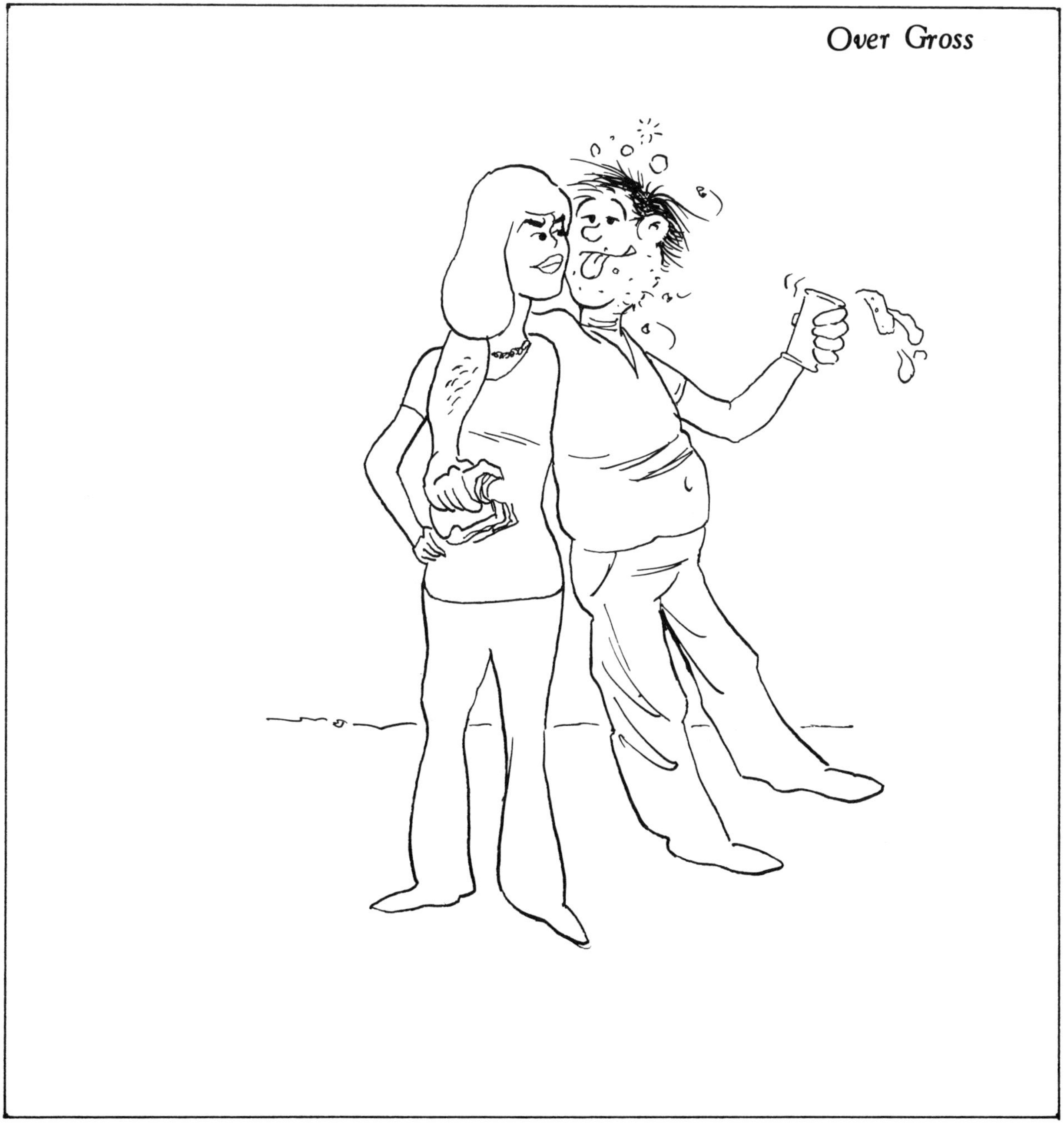
Over Gross

Pack

P

Pack	Any twelve-ounce serving of beer, packaged in groups of six cans or bottles. Not to be confused with a container, which is something like a keg or a pitcher.
Packing Mat	When a skydiver packs his parachute, he first straightens the lines, then brings them all together as he folds the canopy. The folded canopy is stuffed into a little bag, and the next step is to stow the lines in rubber bands. As the lines are stowed, the parachute harness and container are dragged along the ground (or the floor), until the lines are all stowed. This dragging causes unnecessary wear and tear on the harness and container (expensive items, indeed). This is where the packing mat comes in. See, you attach the harness and container temporarily to the packing mat, then when you drag the whole thing across the ground (or floor), only the mat and the suspension lines are subject to wear and tear.
Parachute	Any personnel deceleration device that can be folded up and placed in a container in such a manner that the outcome of its deployment is uncertain. The word is derived from the French words "para," to shield, and "chute," to soil one's underwear. Leonardo da Vinci is credited with the invention of the parachute, and, also to his credit, he was smart enough not to test his idea.

Para-Sailing

Parachute Landing Fall	The Parachute Landing Fall, or PLF, is an ancient landing technique in which the parachutist attempted to compensate, gymnastically, for the inefficiency of equipment designed for military use. Parachutists in the old days wore French boots, motorcycle helmets, practiced PLFs endlessly, and broke lots of bones in spite of all these precautions.
Para-Sailing	Mexican Skydiving. The biggest drop zones are in Acapulco and Cancun.
Para-Ski	As skydiving became safer, and with the softer landings provided by ram-air parachutes, some jumpers began to miss the camaraderie once shared on the weekends with the friendly folks on the rescue squad, and the nurses and doctors in the emergency room. For these jumpers, the para-ski event was created, combining all the fun of parachuting with the social possibilities a compound fracture on the ski slopes can provide.
Paratrooper	A military parachutist. A possible career alternative for the student who is going broke because he can't get off static line. See your Army recruiter, or talk to a Golden Knight.
Partial Inversion	See Mae West. See also Dolly Parton and Lonnie Anderson.

Partial Malfunction	This type of malfunction is called "partial" to distinguish it from a total malfunction, but it's just as bad as a total, or maybe even worse. It doesn't sound so bad; I mean, hey, it's just a *partial* malfunction, right? Wrong! Having a partial malfunction is sort of like being a little bit pregnant, or maybe a little bit dead.
Pee Gravel Also **Pea Gravel**	A kind of gravel, consisting of small, smooth pebbles, used to provide a soft landing area for accuracy jumpers, and named for its color.
Pilot	The jump pilot is usually someone who has just received his commercial license, and is "building hours," which means because of his relative inexperence, nobody will hire him yet, so he's working for free, practicing on you, so to speak. Skydivers understand this, and never hesitate to offer useful tips and suggestions for which the pilot is naturally grateful.
Pilot Chute	The little parachute that drags out the big parachute. I think it was invented by a provencial Roman procurator, around the time of Christ, but I could be wrong about this one.
Pin	A pin is a metal gadget that is passed through a locking loop of fabric to keep a parachute container closed until you throw out your pilot chute. If the pilot chute can't pull the pin out, the pin is said to be locked, the pilot chute is said to be in tow, and the parachutist is said to be in deep shit.

Pin Check	An ancient skydiving ritual in which parachutists once wasted a few seconds on the ground to inspect one another's equipment, possibly saving a life.
Poised Exit	An exit by a lady skydiver who has been to modelling school.
Porosity	This refers to the volume of air that can pass through the fabric of a canopy, and is said to be high, low, zero, or piss poor. For example, a canopy that is for sale at a suspiciously good price probably has high, or piss poor, porosity.
Pro Rating	An advanced demonstration rating that certifies that the holder is capable of making a large annual donation to the United States Parachute Association.

Pin Check

Quick-Ejector Hardware

Parachute snaps that release quickly by simply pulling a lever. These can be used anywhere; for example, they could be used to get rid of an uncooperative tandem passenger, especially one who paid cash in advance.

R

Ram-Air Canopy	A modern gliding parachute with a forward speed in excess of twenty miles per hour. This rams air up the parachutist's nose, hence the term, "ram-air."
Relative Work	Freefall parachuting with one's brothers, sisters, cousins, etc.
Reserve	An auxiliary parachute which the skydiver hopes will open, if his main parachute malfunctions. Since they both work basically the same, lots of luck, and y'all be careful now, you heah?
Rigger	This is the person who packs the reserve parachute. He also inspects the reserve, and can make repairs, if necessary. He is every skydiver's friend, at least three times a year.
Rip Cord	A device for opening the reserve parachute. The rip cord should be discarded immediately after use, and the replacement costs a week's salary which is a rip-off. Hence, the term, "rip cord."
Round	Any parachute that is not square is said to be "round." Square parachutes are really rectangular, but it's much easier to say "square," and everyone knows what you mean. Some parachutes are triangular, but they have not caught on, and will not be discussed further in this dictionary.

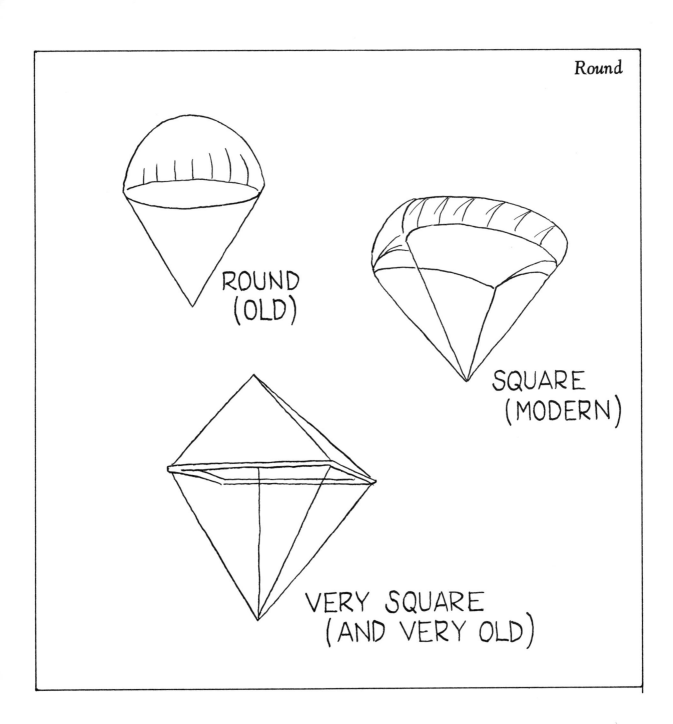

ROUND
(OLD)

SQUARE
(MODERN)

VERY SQUARE
(AND VERY OLD)

Rubber Band	Everybody knows what a rubber band is, but in skydiving, a rubber band is a special, short, fat rubber band that is used to stow the suspension lines. It is made out of a synthetic rubber, uniquely compounded in such a way that it always breaks after two jumps, and always when you are packing, so you have to put down the suspension lines and get another rubber band, and then the lines get all tangled up, but you don't really care, because that's why you've got the reserve, right?
Russian Roulette	(See Base Jumping.)

Rubber Band

S

Seat Belts	Aircraft seat belts are required by the FAA on all jump aircraft, and every parachutist insists on using these safety devices while driving to and from the drop zone.
Sequential Relative Work	If you do relative work, and then you do some more relative work on the same jump, then that's sequential relative work.
Silk	Silk is a natural fiber that comes out of the rear end of a worm. Recently it was discovered that these worms have a low incidence of cancer of the colon, which is why natural fiber is such a hot item in the grocery stores. In the old days, parachutes were made out of silk, because that's all there was. Parachutists just tried not to think about the worms. If a pilot had to make an emergency jump, it was called, "hitting the silk." Somehow, "hitting the nylon" just doesn't have the same ring to it, and today most pilots just say something like, "To hell with it, I'm punchin' out of this fuckin' crematorium!"
Sky God	1. A sky diver who is experienced, highly skilled, and commands the respect of his peers. 2. A sky diver who *thinks* he is experienced, highly skilled, and commands the respect of his peers.

Sleeve	In the old days, round canopies were placed in a long, skinny thing called a sleeve, instead of a deployment bag. That's what a sleeve was, a kind of deployment device. Today, a bag uses about one tenth the material of a sleeve, but costs just as much, or maybe more, than a sleeve used to. Still, a bag is better. You'd feel pretty silly packing a square canopy in a sleeve, just to save a couple of bucks, and it probably wouldn't even work.
Slider	An opening shock inhibitor, the slider controls the deployment of a ram-air parachute by slowly sliding down the suspension lines. If it doesn't slide down the suspension lines, it becomes what the parachutist calls an opening inhibitor. He probably also calls it a few other things, as well.
Slider Bumper	These are little soft plastic tube-like hickeys that you put over your connector links (rapid links) to protect the grommets on your slider, which comes whizzing down and bangs into the connector links. Slider bumpers also protect your head during deployment, and sometimes come loose and slide up the lines, giving you still another opportunity to practice your emergency procedures.

Smoke	Skydivers who make demo jumps like to wear a smoke grenade attached to their feet, so that spectators on the ground can follow them in their freefall maneuvers. The most popular smoke grenade is the military M-18 smoke grenade, which begins to burn when you pull a pin, just like a regular grenade. Sometimes they blow up like a regular grenade, cooking your foot like a roasted frankfurter, but then what's a third degree burn when you're talking about entertainment, the roar of the crowd, etc.?
Spot	1. The local drop-zone mascot. 2. The exit point, as determined by throwing a wind drift indicator. A good spot is important if you want to make it back to the field, on the wind line. Traditionally, a parachutist who lands off target due to his poor spotting returns to announce that the spot has changed, and to demand that another wind drift indicator be thrown. (See Wind Drift Indicator, Lie)
Square	A square is a rectangular shape having four equal sides. (Jesus, I thought everybody knew that.)
S&TA	Safety and Training Adviser. If you ever have a problem with your DZ, TSOs, BOD, WDI, AAD, AFF, USPA, the FAA, FAI, CRW, or the BSRs, see your S&TA, O.K?
Stable	An individual who jumps from an aircraft and falls, face down, without opening his parachute is said to be stable. Why, nobody knows.

Static Line	A nylon line, attached at one end to the aircraft, and at the other end to a parachute, in such a manner that the weight of the parachutist, falling from the aircraft, causes the parachute container to be opened. You'd think they'd call it an opening line, wouldn't you? What the hell does static have to do with anything?
Streamer	A partial malfunction in which the parachute and lines are deployed, but the canopy doesn't inflate. Anyone who has experienced a streamer can tell you that a better name for it would be a "screamer." Sometimes people call a wind drift indicator a streamer, but it's not a streamer, it's a wind drift indicator. Some people are just ignorant, but that's nothing to be ashamed of. Hell, that's why I'm writing this book.
Student	A beginning skydiver who has not yet qualified for his A license, but still has some money left.
Style	1. A competitive event in which a single parachutist, in freefall, performs a predetermined series of maneuvers. 2. To the relative work jumper, a waste of perfectly good altitude.
Suspension Lines	These are the lines that attach the parachute to the risers, and usually are instrumental in causing malfunctions. Military parachutists call them "shroud lines," but what do they know?

T

Take-off Roll	The distance traveled by an accelerating aircraft before it becomes airborne. To compute the take-off roll for a fully-loaded jump aircraft, multiply the length of the runway, in feet, by 1.0.
Tandem Jump	A jump in which an experienced jumper, using large canopies and special equipment, can take a paying passenger along for the ride. (The FAA actually buys the notion that this is a training device!)
Target	The place where skydivers are trying to land. For the accuracy competitor, it is a five-centimeter disc. For the relative worker, it is the county in which the drop zone is located.
Terminal Velocity	1. In skydiving, when you can't fall any faster because of all the air going past, that's your terminal velocity. 2. To the layman, and the rescue squad, terminal velocity is the rate of descent at which a falling body, upon impact with the ground, will be unable to maintain structural integrity, and will therefore be rendered biologically non-viable (terminated), and unlikely to pay any outstanding bills.

Throw-out Pilot Chute	The modern skydiver uses a throw-out pilot chute which is folded up and stowed in a pocket. When he reaches opening altitude, he grabs a cheap plastic handle attached to the pilot chute, pulls the pilot chute from the pocket, and "throws it out." That's where they got the name, see?
Throw-up	This is what the skydiver does when he can't get the goddamned pilot chute out of the little pocket, and/or when he has consumed more than two six-packs of beer in thirty-seven minutes.
Tracking	A freefall body position which increases the rate of descent, the likelihood of collision, and gives the illusion of lateral movement across the sky.

U

U.S.P.A.	The United States Parachute Association, a non-profit, voluntary membership association of skydivers whose purpose is promoting and representing skydiving. As a division of the NAA, it is the official U.S. representative of the FAI but has nothing to do with the CIA, the MIA, the AFL-CIO, or the Teamsters.
Unstable	1. A freefall condition in which the parachutist has lost control of his body position, and tumbles "ass over tea kettle." Some parachutists now call this "freestyle." 2. The mental condition of most skydivers.

V

VFR	Visual Flight Rules. This just means that the pilot can see pretty good if it's VFR, and you don't have to coax or bribe him into flying up through the cloud cover. Sometimes, even if it's very cloudy, the pilot will fly if everybody agrees that conditions are "VFR." Just keep saying things like, "Gosh, this is really great VFR weather, whadda ya say, Freddie boy!"
Velcro	One day in 1948, a swiss inventor was hiking through the Alps. When he came home, he was annoyed to find burdock burrs stuck to his trousers and socks. "Goddammit," he said (in Swiss talk), "I hate these fucking burdock burrs." Years later, he discovered that velcro closures in his clothing would stick to his socks in the clothes dryer. "Goddammit," he said, "I hate this velco almost as much as I hate those fucking burdock burrs." No one knows where velco came from, but modern skydiving would not be the same without it.
Video	The modern equivalent of the old movie camera, a video camera represents the state of the art in freefall movie photography. With a video camera mounted on his helmet, the freefall photographer can show his audience, immediately upon landing, that he missed most of the action.

W

Water Jump	A training jump in which the parachutist quickly learns that if he lands in a body of water, he will most surely drown, especially if it is an *open* body of water.
Whuffo	To tell you the truth, I have never in my life heard a skydiver use this word, but it's always in the books, so here goes: A Whuffo is a non-skydiving individual who, upon witnessing a parachute jump, says, ''Whuffo you jump out of a perfectly good airplane, and whuffo did I just say 'whuffo' when I really meant, 'Why'?''
Wind Drift Indicator	A bright yellow ribbon of crepe paper which, when thrown from an aircraft at opening altitude, just above the target area, drifts with the wind for the approximate duration of a canopy descent, indicating where the jumpers should have opened their canopies eight to fifteen minutes ago, before the wind changed, in order to land on the field. (See Wind Sock.)
Wind Line	An imaginary line extending from the opening point to the target. This means that if you think you are on the wind line, you have a pretty good imagination.
Wind Sock	A device mounted near the pea gravel that clearly indicates to the descending parachutist what the wind direction was before the last 180 degree wind shift.

Water Jump

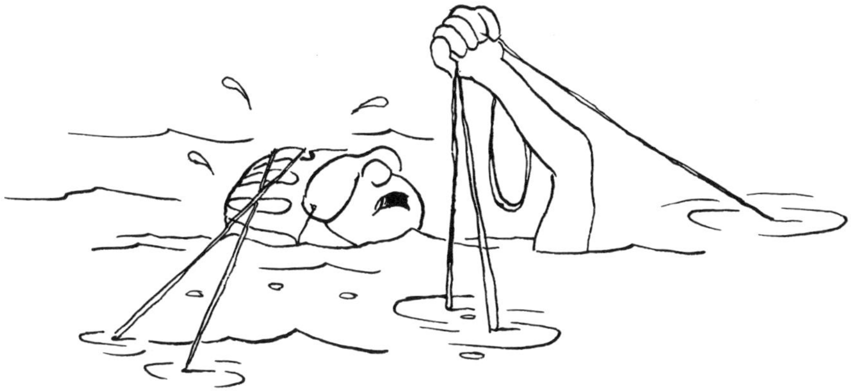

Wind Sock

Wrap   A maneuver performed during Canopy Relative Work (CRW), which provides everyone involved with a valuable opportunity to practice his emergency procedures. It is so named because the parachutist's body is frequently "wrapped" in a fellow jumper's canopy, saving the rescue squad the trouble of draping a blanket over the remains.

X

X-Ray   A medical technique for examining the bones of someone who has just survived a wrap.

Y

Yuppie

The yuppie skydiver can be identified on the drop zone by his passion for excellence in all things that can be purchased, and his shallow sense of what is important. In the evening, he is easily spotted, being the only skydiver who drinks white wine or Perrier instead of beer. In conversation, he will discuss his equipment in terms of investment potential and depreciation.

Z

Zephyrhills   Some place in Florida, included in this dictionary because there aren't too many words that begin with Z.

Zipper   A closing device used on jump suits which always breaks just when you are in a hurry to get into your gear. A broken zipper is impossible to repair, so of course you must buy a new jump suit. Included in this work for the same reason as Zephyrhills.